THE MILLION-PETALLED FLOWER OF BEING HERE

Vidyan Ravinthiran was born in Leeds, to Sri Lankan Tamils. His first book of poems, *Grun-tu-molani* (Bloodaxe Books, 2014), was shortlisted for the Forward Prize for Best First Collection, the Seamus Heaney Centre Poetry Prize and the Michael Murphy Memorial Prize. His second, *The Million-petalled Flower of Being Here* (Bloodaxe Books, 2019), a Poetry Book Society Recommendation, was shortlisted for both the 2019 T.S. Eliot Prize and the 2019 Forward Prize for Best Collection, and won a Northern Writers Award. He teaches at Harvard University in the US, and was previously Senior Lecturer in North American Literature at the University of Birmingham. He is the author of *Elizabeth Bishop's Prosaic* (Bucknell, 2015), winner of both the University English Prize and the Warren-Brooks Award for Outstanding Literary Criticism. On top of his academic work, he writes literary journalism, and is represented as an author of fiction by the Wylie Agency.

VIDYAN RAVINTHIRAN

THE MILLION-PETALLED FLOWER OF BEING HERE

BLOODAXE BOOKS

Copyright © Vidyan Ravinthiran 2019

ISBN: 978 1 78037 476 5

First published 2019 by
Bloodaxe Books Ltd,
Eastburn,
South Park,
Hexham,
Northumberland NE46 1BS.

Second impression 2019.

www.bloodaxebooks.com
For further information about Bloodaxe titles
please visit our website and join our mailing list
or write to the above address for a catalogue.

Supported using public funding by
ARTS COUNCIL
ENGLAND

Cover design: Neil Astley & Pamela Robertson-Pearce.

Printed in Great Britain by Bell & Bain Limited, Glasgow, Scotland, on
acid-free paper sourced from mills with FSC chain of custody certification.

for Jenny

ACKNOWLEDGEMENTS

Poems set wholly in italics are found poems, drawn from the writer named in the title ('Paatti' is Tamil for one's paternal grandmother). 'Clouds, two' is a translation from Jorge Luis Borges, with a bit of Arun Kolatkar spliced in.

I'm grateful to the editors at *PN Review*, *The Poetry Review*, *The Dark Horse*, *The Nation*, *The Yale Review* and *COG* for publishing some of these poems. Two appeared in *The Mighty Stream: poems in celebration of Martin Luther King* (Bloodaxe Books/Newcastle Centre for the Literary Arts, 2018). This collection could not have been completed without the support of New Writing North, and I would also like to thank Liz Kleinman for her intelligence and tact. Sarah Howe and Dai George read the manuscript both kindly and critically; regarding 'Our first house', Dai would have it remembered that Michael Chopra turned out to be a perfectly serviceable Championship striker.

The front cover shows a woodcut of a Leonids meteor storm in 1833 adapted for a Seventh-day Adventist book, *Bible Readings for the Home Circle* (1889); the back cover features an inset portrait by my wife, Jenny Holden.

CONTENTS

We had it before, but then it was going to end,
And was all the time merging with a unique endeavour
To bring to bloom the million-petalled flower
Of being here.

PHILIP LARKIN, 'The Old Fools'

A calf which befriends a pig will also eat muck. But the string that holds together a garland of flowers takes on their fragrance.

TAMIL PROVERB

Today

I was reading my book by the window
waiting for you when I noticed one flower
of those you'd artfully splayed had snapped.
Like a limp wrist the orange gerbera hung, and over
my knuckle it vented a beige gunge. As I snipped
the stem for a smaller vase, the glow
of the radiant petals was too much. Time lapped
me round, the day went unseized.
For this was no opportunity I could have missed;
only the lonely moment which blazed
in my hand, unplucked. Like many,
I had forgotten that time isn't money
and I don't need always to be on the move
within the world you've shown me how to love.

Aubade

It's Saturday but you haven't slept in.
Your side of the bed's still warm.
My hangover is like a smashed windscreen.
I hear a repeated noise down the corridor.
One surface determinedly rubs another.
While asleep I picked my lip till it bled
– a side effect of the medication,
like the gravid if sledgehammer-obvious nightmare.
Your body walks in completely naked.
This is how you prefer to clean the bathroom
and though my plan was for inertia
I understand today we're to redeem the time.
The sound of the curtains yanked apart
is the morning clearing its throat.

Sea break

The horizon was pencilled in then smudged
– what you saw of it was through the sand the wind
drew seaward in a white, chiffony curl.
It was time to have, as they say, a conversation about us
while the air turned gritty as a documentary
and the goldfinch bouncing above the rail
brought back last night and all my lust.
And so we spoke but also watched together
this box-set of astonishing weather:
brown iron rusted to the eye-feel of chorizo;
a shattered packet of basmati rice
floating in with the tide which turned deep taupe
as the gusty beach was throbbing silver
– the elements taking on each other's colour.

Hazlitt

Happy are they, who live in the dream
of their own existence, and see all things
in the light of their own minds; who walk by
faith and hope, not by knowledge; to whom
the guiding star
of their youth still shines from afar,
and into whom the spirit of the world
has not entered!... They live
in the midst of arrows, and of
death, unconscious of harm.
Evil impressions fall off
from them, like drops of water. The yoke of life
is to them light and supportable. The world
has no hold on them. They are in it, not of it.

Frost

said writers (men) could learn
a thing or two from sports – whose jargon
becomes that of business. And war.
Now we live together, we know how. Before,
it frightened me, our day at the US Open.
I thought of how I liked to walk, having
blurted onto the page a line or two,
down the corridor of my solitary flat, and back again
– like Roddick in his final match
seeking the ballgirl's towel after every point,
though his brow looked dry on the giant screen.
Sometimes, I thought, I look out of the window
a few minutes, or hours. – And the next year,
once we'd moved in together?

The armchairs

were ancient and, struck on the bolster,
produced shimmering dust. No matter.
In them we wrote. Side by side and facing out
over the sunlit grounds of the college
we'd soon leave for what they call the *real world*.
(A phrase which means to me the civil war
my parents fled; the women in your
books who grasp the thistle of their lives; and not,
as the hard-nosed mocker of our generation prates,
the necessity of moving to London, and doing a job one hates…)
But there we were, in the meantime, laptops on laps
and wires happily crossed. Where the silver birch goes
for gold and settles for bronze. Then blue.
Then grey. We work so well together – who knew?

Learning

how to be together amid other people;
your hand on my knee beneath the table;
mine, in the curve of your back as we linger,
amiable or disgruntled, at the bar;
the umpteen cues, verbal or non-verbal,
which mean *it's time to leave*, or *could*
we stay; meeting each other's eyes, mid-anecdote,
in a way that isn't public, but remains a shade
raw – appearing in that moment
to exclude our closest friends,
(whose intimacies leave us cold)
we tease each other to placate the room,
mocking our love's deepest movements,
returning to the world we all assume.

Jigsaw

Dumping the pieces on a faded yoga mat,
on all fours you scrutinise the chaos;
you, who enjoy watching snooker because
'it's like tidying up', and squint along the grease-defaced
counter like a sniper down her scope, to purge it of crumbs.
You've got yourself into this mess
and your intensity – as if doing sums
in your head – is a courageous waste
of energy, for one who, like me, can't cease
but must be tinkering forever with the universe:
a small and private achievement, a renewing,
a collapse of ambition into local doing;
though I know you're sleeping badly, waking bleak
for worries about your latest book.

Riposte

You scan my work for where I don't make sense.
I edit yours to make what's quiet in you loud.
Neither's gift's secure. I'm not proud
of being opaque to you. Since
you've let yourself down, writing, as Hopkins put it,
on and from the level of your own mind, timidly
I add comments in Word and temper with praise;
hedge; linger, like a bad reviewer, on the similes.
(We like to link, in our writing, unlike things – that's no surprise.)
Then I wait for your call, or in the other room, depending on whether
this happens when we're apart, or together.
You're quick to give in: did you know already this wouldn't work?
This is one of the ways we love and hurt each other.
The rewrite lets me off the hook; I praise with envy and relief.

Fiction

Though I've never been one for the archives
I want there always to be more of you to know.
When you complain I've heard it all already
I ask like a child for the old story
or for you to make something up. Now
you say you found in a drawer one day
– as a girl – the love letters of your parents,
which you read with envy
thinking you would never be loved.
This isn't a prompt, or grateful; a request
for reassurance. It's fact, not fiction.
The letters, I ask desperately.
Were they bound with a ribbon?
Were there locks of hair?

Hail

Down the corridor comes the sound
in lovely spasms – you, typing; I know that strain
like freak summer hail (it's June) clattering the pane.
Once – it was years ago, winter – I'd stand
after you dropped off and I couldn't
on the landing of another house we didn't own,
beneath the skylight at the top of the stairs,
looking up where nothing could be seen
and also heard: rain, sleet; hail; wind, hail, rain.
Then walk – at the beginning, of you and me –
back and forth in the dark to learn
the way home to your sleeping body. A game
of being alone and not in a strange place
you're playing now, determined not to lose.

Nothing can be sole or whole...

We have been lucky. For each place we rent
– unable to buy, work, write, live, somewhere permanent –
a field has been following us.
No sooner have we knifed free
one more paint-jammed window
above a broken loo
than we're carried by our own legs
past rhubarb torn to giant, seething tatters; hoof-pocks
in dry mud; thistles and butterflies tinting the path
beneath the sky-vexing pylon
– into green, unurgent space. Where
you couldn't fly a kite between the sizzling wires
yet another year
renews its mellow rain and biting sun.

Ceylon

– the word's on the tip of your tongue
(or, as you say it, *tong*), as we take tea.
Waiting for you to speak, I sip mine:
Tetley's tastes of nothing, but I suppose
it's good to know true flavourlessness,
the prose of life we sugar over with verse.
*Cey*lon you say – a trochee not an iamb –
referring to the drink I drink
with two spoonfuls at home and, here, none.
Though by 'home', I mean the house
my parents live in and where I grew up;
like, and unlike, them saying 'back at home'
when they intend Sri Lanka, and not Leeds
where they live and I haven't, not for years.

DH1

The flat was opposite a nightclub.
Yelling, vomit, and the bass. We couldn't sleep
but made the best of it. One evening,
early evening, warm from a crucial nap
we heard a noise and looked down from
the Juliet balcony, on the gamboge courtyard.
It was the longest day of summer. A fellow with a beard
and a dishdasha – the kind of man I fear
my Hindu dad would call a *bloody kaka* –
held the controls, as hither and thither
the red-black drone whirred through the air.
After it waddled his happy toddler,
round-faced and uncertain as a kitten
lightly tortured, lovingly, with a piece of string.

Our first house

we lost in months when the owners chose to sell.
To buy it ourselves was only improbable.
It's tough but we're luckier than many.
The mortgage would be reasonably unreasonable;
over the years we'd find the money.
But in that area no one smiled at us;
we learned not to and to walk past quickly.
Each conversation with the neighbour
with whom we shared a wall and nothing else
was clenched as the talk of a stranger
trapped briefly with you in a lift or the aisle
of a packed train. We were the only renters.
The lads in their car yelled *Chopra* – racist, I suppose,
given his abysmal record for the Magpies.

A gift

The brown-black-white cat from next door
laid to rest on the rubber prickles of our doormat
a rainy, fine-haired, grey-brown mouse. It
purred, the cat, and yearned upward as we left
or entered that house, like a small fist
its sleek head punched upward and was defused
by a strong caress. Which gave the wrong signal
for why else bring us her soaked kill? She,
the cat, used to hide from you and me
in the wet hedge. Strange she'd now annex
to her domain of scents the place we lived, ourselves alone.
Would she ever learn, like the rest, to be happy
taking only what is given, at our prickly border
of absent-minded... – Would you call it affection?

You've been teaching me

the names of birds. The commonest
were strange to me – one of those gaps that go
unremarked within the immigrant child. Flying the nest
he thrills to what he doesn't know
as your white hand tells apart the bluetit from the coaltit
jabbing at the peanut feeder in the garden
we rent from a woman who looks at
one of us only when she talks. That jot
of colour in grey Durham's a wagtail
probing a kobicha cobble and when
the tide crests with a sigh the distant pier
at Tynemouth it's time for our in-joke
about the exotic whimbrel I make
of every common, straight-billed curlew.

BAME

A mixed-race couple sat on the couch
watching, on TV, a mixed-race
couple on the couch. She's white, he's black.
My brother-in-law, the ad-man: 'The public
finds black people cool.' I would parse
– an actor of my hue – as a humorous
Apu figure only, or a terrorist... No wonder my face
in the mirror feels unlikely – what channel is this?
Since what we're exposed to shapes what we desire
I wonder at the Muslim boy in your class
growing up, his curly hair's taboo allure.
You longed to touch (he wasn't your friend)
– do I follow in his footsteps? And how to understand
my unfading passion for your pale skin?

Thought experiment

If I love you can I love everyone,
even the stranger reading this page
in a place, a light, out of reach? A person
who has survived the silent purge
of those who don't share our tastes, skin,
politics – though no one who's made it this far
through a book of poems could differ
so much… But I can only love you.
Must the rest be tolerance, or administration?
Thugs in the riots sniffed the oil
in men's hair to check, were they Tamil.
Victims were pulled close in a strange intimacy
and then embraced by a burning tyre.
Contamination; fellow feeling; guns for hire.

An email

about – good word – a *fractious* morning:
walking in, the first you heard from Carole
is she's read your stories, doesn't like them:
'there's no beginning and no end!' The world
doesn't owe us love. But we can't be everything
to each other, needing someone out there
who understands – Yeats imagined his cold
stanzas nestled in the warm ear of a fisherman.
My uncle, fired at and imprisoned, suffered more,
no doubt, struggling through my first collection.
Until he'd made something of every poem
he wouldn't yield. My novel about Sri Lanka
wasn't published: still in his hot flat
he wrote to me of what it meant to him.

In this room

you've a tiny minority, who in this space,
this parochial space, feel their passion
is of some consequence. Each person
says they're different. So it's a race
to be the first, or most, while also being loved.
Outside this room their voice
may not carry. There's the internet, of course
– likes at a remove. I pushed and shoved
to bring you here, and feel your hate
towards the vanity, the spite, the predictable intonation
of those like me. You scrutinise the tea-light
like a lonely child – as if it held the secret.
I'm sorry, too. Let's rebuild somewhere quiet
with emollient mockery our club of two.

Children say the funniest things

Watching *Cool Runnings*, you cringe to remember
I'm freezing my royal Rastafarian nay-nays off
– how your parents froze, embarrassed
by their child's quotation. I'm silent now
instead of laughing, which worries you
but I'm only remembering how
as a child I felt stared at and wished – out loud,
to my mum, as if she might
grant my wish – that I was snow-white.
I tell you instead about my nephew,
who, confused by the gay couple next door,
asked if he and his brother could live together
one day, like those two grown men.
And then we begin to talk about children.

There are things

you know that I can't feel – and the other way round.
Insults are yelled at me I hate for you to hear.
The boss jokes about ejaculating on you at the place you volunteer.
We take it in turns to say *you can't understand*,
then take it back, believers in the imagination.
Of course you can, I can, despite what happened
or did not, to either. When my sister's husband's mum
first took my golden nephew to the park
another child wasn't allowed to play with him
– she assumed the worst. It was for her
like growing out of her chest a third, mixed-race arm
naked and haemophiliac and liable
to be punched. Now each of us requires new armour,
and ways besides love of taking it off.

Sometimes

when you tell me what happened
there's a strong light in your eyes that shimmer
with what must be tears but don't fall – and
the anger lends quiet you a hurtling grammar.
You are alive in your opposition.
It reminds me of Sidney Poitier
when he's called *boy* and slapped and then
slaps back – instinctively – which is a sign
he's intact although the glare he foists
on his foe is made of tears. By which I mean
you see in his eyes how much it costs. The armour's
off – unsure what to say, I stick the kettle on
for Sidney Poitier, who removes her boots with a groan
and changes, upstairs, her pencil dress for pyjamas.

Who am I

and what can I get away with, or from
is the question we're asking
this rainy weekend, when we should be multi-tasking,
shopping online or working from home.
There is no need, given the quality of the light,
and the conversations we've had,
to ask each other: 'What are you thinking?';
episodes remain, and will disappoint
only slightly; at a loss, we could fight,
given what one heard, or misheard.
'I am powerful and no longer a victim,' goes the harangue
while others nod, with furrowed brows – listen, or don't;
'You must fall silent before my wound,
which, as in Shakespeare, has the truest tongue.'

No

that isn't a poem, I suppose,
about me and the woman I love – or it's both
that and a magic trick with pronouns
I go on trying with a periodic faith
because I would love you
to, as, in your mind, these words pronounce
themselves, feel kin; and not step back, either in revulsion,
or saying 'I sympathise, but cannot understand,
being, by society, differently-skinned.'
I am – imagine her speaking, if you prefer –
tired of appearing in your eyes
posed like a strongman (or Rosie the riveter)
or shackled, bloodied, on the floor:
I would look into your eyes and speak. And listen.

Leeds

– where my parents live and I place in my mouth
with a fork and not my hand a polygon
of potato which has swum for hours amid lamb on the bone,
coconut milk, black mustard and fennel seeds.
You're in Wiltshire. We speak on the phone
as I leave the cul-de-sac, past where
the nice houses are; down the oak-dark lane,
through the crossroads, and to the Norman church
with its arch of hewn aboriginal stares. Long distance
means talking every day with nothing to share;
my emails are try-hard. Lolloping
out of the daffodils in the pink light, I see a hare,
moving exactly like a faster creature
in slow motion. I wish you were here.

In my father's room I discover

among the Wilbur Smiths and icons for pooja
W.C. Lefroy's *The Ruined Abbeys of Yorkshire*.
Its blood-red leather's like a sari;
only the spine is worn by the touch of the air
to the colour of your shoulder-blades when we
forget sun cream abroad. 'Like the sound of brave words
or fine music in dreary scenes and moments of depression
is the sight of Kirkstall Abbey', writes the author,
'in the purlieus of dim, laborious Leeds.' We've been,
of course, but did you know my parents took me as a teen
to see *Hamlet* performed in the ruins?
We brought green bean and potato curry in buns,
a thermos of hot lemon; crisps, as provoking of tuts
as my dad flipping through his York Notes.

Peak District

The lambs wore fuchsia digits; wisps
of torn cloud hung from beech roots and barbed wire.
Close boles fused. Why were we here?
To flee our inboxes. To peer,
half-cut, down a blue road, hunting
pockets of signal. After killing the bottle,
it became possible
to say and do wonderful things to each other.
A quip from our guide, concerning
the light and dark Peaks; a biddie glowered
in her one-street village from her stone bench. You drove
fast and sure, round the lake clouds turned mauve
before they swung apart and we faced the glitter
like cameras flashing in a stadium crowd.

Clouds, two *(Borges feat. Kolatkar)*

Through the air walk placid peaks,
a day-darkening *cordillera*. But these are clouds
with odd shapes. An *explosion of cheeks*,
said Kolatkar – Shakespeare saw a dragon
in a flamy cloud akin to this which floats
like a remembered word across the afternoon.
– Across oceans, those of time, too. But
this vision, is it real, and was it the same
for all of us; and what are clouds, anyway? A form
of chance; a warning to or from
God, connected with his infinite scheme
that goes fuzzy, so we lose the thread.
Maybe the cloud's as conscious of her meaning
as the man gazing at her, come morning.

Leviathan

We would like to believe that, like the lovers
in Donne, we rule a kingdom of two
in our panic room. That as the body recovers
after love the sun which burns through
our blissed-out eyelids cannot dent us.
But the script intrudes and domination enters;
your phone is flashing with a work email;
our jobs aren't safe and we still rent. The struggle
is to house share with Leviathan – while
amending the lines we're given and that do arouse,
that we've been sold and we're sold on,
with moments wholly ours to improvise…
Hobbes, on anxiety: a *perpetual solicitude*
of the time to come. The happiest moment must erode.

That said

after being ignored, or stared at,
misspelled or mispronounced; and not
by the simply wrongfooted, but
those who act as if I concocted my name
or face just to be difficult – as I might write a poem –
it is everything, to be desired. To, in bed,
on my side, on my side, mellow
while your hand and voice compares to a cello
my curving flab. The first time I saw you rise
naked from the sheets there was the surprise
of your olive skin. That was before
I learned of your granny from Greece
who escorted English soldiers as their cover
until the day she really took one as her lover.

She

doesn't like men with beards – I've forgotten
to shave – each time we meet she's lost
all sense of who we are. We must regain her trust,
begin to know her from the start. There's a pattern:
eventually she smiles and hands you an object.
That's how the baby gives you all her toys.
She doesn't seem to want anything in return.
Each time we visit our friends' house
her face has grasped a new expression.
Our parents at our age had children. We want them, but are
financially – and in other ways – insecure.
Her almost-smile looks for something
in me beyond this lame voice saying *hello there…*
what are these distances to which we cling?

She

reminds me of the immigrant life
– adaptive, wrongfooted, in doubt, and debt;
cliché-clutching, stoical, pervious –
lived joyously by my cousin and his wife
in Nova Scotia. The first time we met
Dhammi had little English but would use
straight away in a sentence each new word
she was keen to learn and not forget.
Now she works in a bank and her idioms arrive on the dot.
Science hasn't given them children yet;
a torment for the Hindu with her sense of fate
but to be fearless and immediate
in a strange, cold, country means giving birth
to oneself every day – and with every breath.

The Indian grandfather

comes between us on date night – as surely as a chaperone.
I fume, ignoring you. We read about his case
and then forgot. Now my phone says the police
officer, whose football tackle paralysed him,
was cleared of excessive force. Though anyone
can see in the video from the dash-cam
what happened to the suspicious 'black guy'
the caller said was around 'thirty' – in reality
a fifty-seven year old visiting Alabama
to care for the baby while his son finished his degree.
'He don't speak a lick of English.' Nope.
Still they bark repeatedly to get up.
The Gordian knot of his dead legs is cut. We recognise
the cop's own posture – a scolded little boy – gauche, powerless.

John Addington Symonds

When I arrived at Woolner's, the maid supposed I was 'for the gentlemen'.
In the dining room, I relapsed into an armchair.
They were talking about the Jamaica business,
Gladstone bearing hard on Eyre,
'that evidence wrung from a poor
black boy with a revolver at his head!'
Tennyson did not argue. He kept asserting.
'We are too tender to savages; we are more
tender to a black than to ourselves. Niggers
are tigers; niggers are tigers.'
It is hard to fix the difference
between the two men, both with a strong provincial accent.
Gladstone's hands are white and not remarkable.
Tennyson's are huge, unwieldy, fit for moulding clay or dough.

Lingerie

A woman and a man. A white body and a brown.
Are we here to remind each other
who we are, or make it possible to forget?
The skin around your eyes is silvery
and in each iris lurks a fleck of red like an ember.
Shadows, perfume, elastic. Your *looped and windowed sides.*
Tiny bows which can't be undone. Purple,
like the word itself – that's Frenchified
for our delectation, like *people*
of colour, or the prose of Oscar Wilde.
MADE IN CHINA. By machines, or the dead-eyed,
repeating one motion? A placeless moan.
The storm has passed. The clouds blush to remember.
When you act, the changes are strong-willed.

Safe words

The verbs tell. What line is crossed
between saying *you give me an erection*,
and *you make me hard*? Jon Silkin:
'many liberals don't just
make love, they first ask each other.'
Is the bedroom a safe space
in which to discover in the face
of the one you love unspoken
forces? This is where contracts are broken
and made; where games are played that are
not games, that have a deep root in our public life. Here
the whip hand does requests and it thrills to listen,
like a safecracker with an ear to the device,
gently moving his fingers until the door swings open.

Don't stop

Now for something completely different.
Let's put euphemism to its true use.
Moving forward is impossible. I am *in a bad place*.
The wind tears at the washing on the line,
bright blowing sleeves. I don't feel like a man
in scrubs at three am could have the answers.
But how kind he was, apologising
for the slow, heroic machine
of the NHS. And October sunlight's a precious thing.
The crying is frequent, unoccasioned.
I don't know what has happened.
I worry this is a confessional poem.
If I don't work, who am I? But I am
still alive, which may come in handy. And so are you.

i.m. Steve Hilton

Unmanageable tears. I think
of Steve, my mum's dead best friend
who cried when his hearing went and he had
to retire. With salt-and-pepper squid on the end
of his laughing fork in that Thai place
all brushed steel and glimmering glass,
he spoke of books to draw me out. *If no one dies
in the first chapter, it's not for me!* Besides my mother,
how many was he always there for,
before and after his diagnosis with cancer
of the liver? Steve was tender to the diminished
as to himself, and never confused pain with value. He cherished
the undramatic beauty of a life that's left
out of the fast-paced thrillers that he loved.

Outside the Hanuman temple

in the sweating foothills of Ramboda,
our round guide serene as the Buddha
said to wait, and for claustrophobic hours we did,
among countless locals awaiting the god
– the measly monkey statue carried aloft.
I don't notice at the time, but you were stared at.
By men with dark ovals at their underarms.
By women holding garlands. By children and the old.
To be respectful, you wore a long flowing dress.
No one there, including me, looked like you
so they looked at you, mingling
swift glances and that shameless, long,
unbroken stare. It's shameful that I didn't notice
what it was like for you in that place.

I mention it

because you're not like that, and now
I'm glad one moment and sad the next,
you see it all. You read me like a book. You text
from work, and it's like the touch of your mouth
on my cheek. It has *the reciprocity of tears* – your mirth.
In this northern city I've been stared at – we have,
for being together. But your eye on me
becomes what keeps me safe; your love
is watchful, analytic, soft and hard. It can be
terrifying to be known so well. There were times
we argued and I refused to speak,
or I went to you and in my embrace
your body was inert, I had to lift your arms
around my neck. Now I live by your first move.

Parental advice

Because you are so intelligent and so special
you can quickly reach a plane
where in your colleagues' minds you are their kind of man
but actually you're separate and looking down
on them – just get on with it... When people
are talking rubbish you should think
about your next project – you should
know exactly where you'll be in the next five years.
You are not one of them. You will have
to be twice as good as they are to achieve
what people in this country take
for granted – but if we are saying the wrong thing
please forgive us we are not intelligent
as you are but we love you

Worry

isn't doing something about the problem
– train yourself out of these thoughts. So
they say. But I think of my dad
coming upstairs to ask in his quiet, sad
voice, 'Can we leave in ten minutes for the station,'
even though it's an hour till my train
back to you, and he doesn't want me to go.
His father's fists turned him mild as a Jain
to his son, me. A boxing champion,
he'd jog in his crop-top round the lagoon
hunting snakes. Then he flew here alone. No wonder
our tribe is of the worrier caste, thinking always
of the vanished countries of the past and future
– to draw a line between, and know that we abide.

I've noticed something

– we both peter out when speaking,
saying *but I don't know*, or something. Why?
In your family talk is for the jousting men:
you write. You listen. You read. You step back from an opinion,
always, as if saying – *why bother? I could be wrong.*
Which I don't think of as being shy:
you simply haven't the need, to set the world to rights, of a man.
And what of my own habit, of cutting myself off, less
out of fear I'm talking crap, than just in case
I won't be understood? I was the special son:
bigged-up, hot-housed, second-generation
precocious; unique, and, therefore, alone.
For what we've both learned is how not to threaten,
how not to seem to know more than our place.

Conversation

Bleakly, there seem two options only.
Sat beside each other, we're both lonely.
The patriarch presides, speaking of economics.
Or like wildfire there glows, in that space
each soul immures, a ragged half of talk. A voice
whose sad ironic echo has neither gravity nor grace.
The rational daylight of the IKEA uplighter
gives way to the darkness of a silent disco.
We're dancing to our private music, when the
devices fail, and, limned by their glow,
all those silent flailing bodies look absurd. Mimics.
You gesture in that vacuum for another shot.
But we've fallen through the floor and off the grid
and your face tells me mine is dead.

The fight

is conventional from beginning to end,
and necessary. It's where we recognise
each other. What, exactly, happened?
We don't agree. It's hard to speak. There are sighs
instead of words, as occasioned
in the speech of those with autism. You cry
look at me: refusing pity, I race
my rage into the other room. My careful words
you've twisted into judgement. *We recognise
each other* – a phrase from a book – did I really say
that? No, we fight with ghosts. Parents, siblings,
some false idea of what a man or woman really is
– they crowd the room. I shoulder through,
ignoring their fell glares and seeking only you.

Afterwards

The rhythms of normalcy.
Light touches, growing stronger. A halo
of goodwill round each remark. We flow
from kitchen to couch, from laughter into memory;
mock the ads together, and the shit TV.
The details of our days bear so much weight,
a tender weight, in this eggshell-lovely phase.
You're more than usually aware of germs.
You're always the first to apologise.
Something has to be done about this. I promise
to try. We order in. Now the only games
we play are with pads in our hands, howling
at the screen. But I'll stop here. For how can the rhythms
of normalcy come alive in poems?

Larkin

It's strange to think his words are strange to you
– lines I grew up with and which grew
on me. Though it's you who like him
wake in the dead of night to the thought of death.
Is this what my students mean by 'relatable'?
His smirking letters don't faze
me, but I wonder at that wild *white* face
his ambulance retrieves from every place.
'Smells of different dinners,' but no coloureds, in 1961...
'Drunk pub wisdom,' a first year said.
Reading to you that racist's words in bed
I float with his genius from 'you' to 'we' – as if
it were in the poet to speak for all of us
of a national – a human? – loneliness.

The poem of happiness

isn't written yet – it talks too much
about places, people, concerning whom
one feels compelled to care. It strikes a match,
goes for a walk in the park, a peachy glow,
gleams like advertising for a culture
that descends on thought's corpse like a vulture.
There's dolour outside the frame
which can't migrate into the poem
of our lives – its true enclosed colour
alien to white sculpture admired for its ratio;
or the photograph by Diane Arbus
of a boy, his rictus, the claw he has made
of his hand, the grenade; or Nick Ut's
napalm-fleeing girl, naked, not nude.

Strictly

– hard to live up to, on Saturday night. I mean
the frictionless assimilation
of sundry cultures – a sparkly cult
insisting on their joy and asking why
anyone must leave. Watching millionaires *on a journey*,
I sense my face when you glance over fail in its smile
for we've drunk too much, or not enough, and I'm too full
of the thought of the passing weekend and the time we while
away on the couch, both together and not. The time we kill
with irony and ritual. Sometimes we embrace
the spirit of the age – ordering, for instance, many takeaways.
Sometimes we're ashamed and to save face
try hard to like what we're given. As if it were us
grinning at the camera, not allowed to not be joyous.

Titian

puts a church in the background, and, closer-to,
these mallowy babes Cupid climbs. Innocence
wounded into sex. Now they see as we do
two lovers with three flutes. A woman and a man
looking at each other with real desire
– where else do you find that, in the art of the Renaissance
or anything since? I don't know if they're
about to begin or have completed their duet.
We can look, and look, at their eyes,
the skin around them and the space between their bodies,
satisfy ourselves it's only paint; and still be left
wondering and achingly outside what they have.
The allegory is a lie; neither we nor anyone else are the same;
we glimpse but cannot grasp their love.

Paatti

Dawn. Darkness is done with, gone from the earth.
The sun's red face
makes the shapeless
once again distinct. Foliage, smothering the path;
the kanaka flowers, like
painted cups amid a tiny forest
– as one corolla withers, there bursts
the next from its green spike.
The achieved bloom has learned to seduce;
the closed bud just below
goes untouched even by the shadow
of an insect. 'Just a leaf,' the bee says.
Today's flame shrivels. But why make a fuss?
The flower of tomorrow is yet to open.

Today

I was stuck for words, then spoke with your voice.
I heard myself laughing in the twilight;
but that was you, on the phone.
We finish each other's sentences, even when alone:
with strangers – and not by choice –
I have been you, and you, me. We've taught
each other ways of being afraid, and open.
Given the moment of dusk on the plum tree,
the pegs on the line tying it to the house
is this tingling gesture mine? This anxiety
I can't escape without your idiom
passed securely down the generations, in this country
– what have I to give you but the eerie spice
of a conversation less defined than home?

Brexit

At Durham station we glance from face to face,
guess how each voted. Later
you see a white man square up to a brown, pass
it on and ask *should I have mentioned that*?
It seems to me my Facebook friends down south are mad
at finding themselves, all of a sudden, a minority
in their own country. Their conventional snobberies
concerning where I live are of a piece
with isms they'd disclaim. You work for the university
alongside women who did not go to university,
who hail from Pity Me and Killhope
and would Leave. All our talk now has this shape:
at lunch a colleague tells me of her mother
who always orders food she cannot bear.

Leave

It makes me ache, how you've written your name
on the front of your leave card for work.
The letters aren't joined up. Each has a firm,
careful shape. This isn't how you jot
notes, letters, shopping lists. Something's missing
from this earnest hand which must be how you wrote
those two proud words on every exercise book
at school. I've heard each anecdote
your parents tell. I know you were premature;
I've seen the photographs, in chronological order,
of the baby, the toddler, the teenager, that you were.
So why is it this earnest script that leads me back
into the life-before-me of my fiancée?
It's knowing that child is alive in you today.

In the mixed area

where my parents live there opens a Sardinian trattoria.
I read in one of their tea-stained tabloids
a rant to mock with you on the phone
– about *Thomas the Tank Engine*.
The new film will include a Chinese train. An Indian train,
a girl. Only the last sentence admits
Gordon, Percy, and the rest will remain: our favourites
will keep their jobs. My nephew – think of his name as *growl*, without the *g* –
was the biggest fan at the age of three.
I remember how afraid he was when he
– Thomas – went off the rails. Then, running his toy along the radiator,
the boy invented a game of angry delight. A towel
tumbled the train to the ground. 'YANSHIDE!' yelled Rahul.
I love my nephew in his big house in Ilkley and his golden mixed-race skin.

Inspiration

On the train, another complains
of Eastern Europeans
with great vigour and spontaneity.
An overflow of powerful feelings.
Her quiet friend vanishes, but for her
atom of polite assent,
an iterated, needless murmur.
The tirade has the scintillating
onwardness of Shelley,
in the form he took
from Dante and his vulgar tongue
into English where it doesn't belong,
is insecure
and beautiful without footholds.

Mercy invincibility

We're playing *Super Mario*. This level's
designed for one player and not two.
The quick-collapsing platforms mean one always falls.
But when he hits the spikes he starts to flash.
The plumber turns invincible as a firewalker.
A chance to extricate oneself. How often
have our lives known that brief
immunity – the crisis which emits
a stretch of ardent unreflective life?
It's afterwards that hurts. Time salts all wounds.
You come to realise: that really happened.
But first there's a quick flick of the stick
as you leap my glimmering sprite between the spikes
and urge me onwards through a wall of fire.

Another side effect

is that I see how beautiful you are and don't
do anything about it. The pang that has
me draw you close has quietened.
Not only that, but I don't feel the loss.
The provocation of your body used to be enough.
Now I'm unhurried, when push comes to shove.
Slowly you remind me there's a line to cross.
Every time means rediscovering the act.
They only argue who cannot seduce;
I've no answer to your perfumed tact
and then I do. With equivocations we cut loose;
how could I forget the way you feel?
I know you'd rather have the chase
which ends against a wall. This is something else.

In my family

it overwhelms, goes viral, we race
to be both first and last, the one who says
I love you most. She insists, my mother,
that you're exactly like her. She bookends her cries
with your name. Each of your brothers
feels blue till the other turns red: their perduring tiff
concerns art, economics, not just desserts
but quiche portion-sizes too. Should love be tough
to prepare a child for the world, or is
family not the world, but a voice
saying forever that we're more than enough? Your mum
lingers, leafing through the album
on photos of the one Greek relative
– sunburnt, moustached – who showed her any love.

Unlike some

others – of no uncertain terms –
I do trust those who struggle with my names.
The lady in the dry cleaner's, for instance,
saying *I'll need you to spell that out, pet!*
Am I to believe this kindly Geordie is a bigot?
Her humour in this common circumstance
is as bright-shining a part of civilisation
as the David's chiselled, white, not-quite fist;
as the shattered porcelain of Miłosz
or your tribe's habit of, in the post-prandial hush,
endlessly offering each other cups of tea;
or the tactful cheatsheet typed up by my family
for my sister's wedding, from which I'd finally learn
my own name's correct, Tamil, pronunciation.

From the window

I can see the gate creak open, and you enter
along the tip-tilted path plants on either side
sling rainy green across. That's when you encounter
the big, inopportune, wet, pink, rose,
brushing it aside with a look that's sad.
Seeing I don't know what in your face,
I go halfway only – a thing unprecedented –
down the stairs, waiting on the latch,
you breathing hard... I can't bear
it any longer – sprinting to surprise
you, I'm rebuffed. It's as if you know
the secret of my pausing on the step,
my lonely fear of being brushed off
as your hand did that shining flower.

That hand

I saw lift – as if to fend off too much light –
at the end of a walk in the park and out of it years ago
once we'd left through the rust-torn gate with its dewy wire.
You paused to look into a golden field;
the resistless softness, of your stopping there!
The hi-vis jackets of police fluoresced
where families unpacked their rugs before
the lunar blank of a projector screen. We kept on
across the tracks. The footbridge blazed as we trod
its vermilion mesh and stared down the rails
towards the horizon – each fiery sleeper
a handhold for our eyes to climb
and when at last the train burst through our legs
the driver waved almost before you'd time to raise your hand.

We're

apart and staying with our parents,
one up North and one down South. On the phone
I mention the park and a drunken yawp and know
you need to hear, given the situation
we find ourselves in, whether it was harmless.
(It must be even here I'm tough to place.)
After we passed, someone he was
with said, laughing, 'Until I saw the look on his face
I thought you must be friends.' And if he's listening in
the lad should know that he and me, like
you and I, were and are in true proximity;
that I too find it hard, stumbling in public
to not glare back – as if on behalf of the nation –
at the innocent pavement in a spirit of accusation.

And so

there are these moments of unease
when words go astray in the familial noise
even though your parents don't care about race
and I've never been torn, like the kind of brown face
that appears in films, between tradition and the West.
Trying to follow what the English mean by class,
the tiny jokey disapprovals – as if an irritation danced –
in the middle of the sitting room I'm lost
trying to follow this conversation about a scone
and how the word should be pronounced.
Before I met you I'd never eaten one
– though I was familiar with this debate
from Basil Bunting's coat-trailing note
to *Briggflatts*, which I left crumby with barota.

from the Tamil

My father Englishes for me the song
he croons but can't place. Which I fudge:
She's the one who if she spoke my language
would make it honey-sweet; the melodic phrase
that loses its meaning on the page
– the flowering vine they say smiles at the moon.
Her fruity lips offer me their juice
and when it's drunk, she looks down shyly.
Lost in translation – within a pronoun –
she's the moonlight that shines inside the jungle where no one is,
the rain that falls on the sea where it isn't needed;
the poem, the thought, which nobody wrote, or had.
Did she grow out of the words in a book
or like the garland of sevanthi flowers, the red lotus born of the mud?

Let

the lamp's pale warmth illumine
the bobbles of your t-shirt for sleep
like the dots of light in a Vermeer, seen close-up.
Water flashes from your skin
the towel leaves pink. With a touch you keep
rearranging the table I have laid.
What do you want? A man said:
they don't know what they want, women
– if only we could live so open to surprise;
uncertain of ourselves, able to change! Please
tell me. If you speak up I will hear
the world out to the end. I'm over the moon,
the sea, the sky. I want you only. No one else
goes without saying. But I mean nothing else.

Dubrovnik

I watch you swim far out from my deckchair,
a black dot amid white glitter. Later,
you insist I reverse down the ladder
slowly – where you leapt in. But the odour,
the giant freeze of the sea and its gross judder
– which I describe, but could never prepare for,
once you've climbed out, you don't remember –
kept me paddling tamely by the shore
grasping the rungs of my own ribs. In Sri Lanka,
the tide licked icily up and over
my bitten legs in the sun-smitten sand – my mother,
hating it, snatched me away before
I was pulled in and under and lost forever.
Yours, when she swam out to sea, took you with her.

Trust

is the problem I think – I don't know
the sea's white fires despite their beauty
will buoy for longer than a fluskering
moment the cage of my brown body.
You hold me in one place so
I can laugh at the sky whose blaze like the salt sting
forces my eyes shut, then set me free
to lunge back to what feels safe and clasp the rung.
I'm too concerned about myself to let go
of this alert and visceral anxiety
until we creep that night past the blazing
fusion restaurant into the humid trees
to love each other in a hurry
on solid ground and on our knees.

My body is a cage

We're streaming Arcade Fire's original.
Someone remarks in their comment
it could be an anthem for trans people.
There follows an extended argument
when someone else objects the song's for everyone.
I never said it wasn't, X tries to explain.
But it's in Y's blood to go on and on.
Without the inbuilt amiability, or cowardice
which softens a conflict face-to-face
we're looking at an abstract rage,
a typed-out feeling of having something
taken away. The song, one thinks, can't be mine
and also manage to belong
to this person who isn't me. For *my body is a cage*.

Transition

We love those who twist and don't stick
with givens, who won't simply give back
to others what others leap to recognise;
and we love characters, like those
in Dickens, who are always, loveably, the same:
but, walking down North Road, past the ailing
grocer, the long-closed Globe cinema, turned Chinese
buffet, by way of bingo hall, now derelict,
how can I explain to you what happened
when I asked the powers that be if they'd looked
into what was said – concerning race?
Hems and haws replaced their spoken prose.
The language of HR became a carapace. Who
were these evasive strangers I thought I knew?

Tough mudder

Back when my sister, as Salome, made parents cry,
our lot's joke was that she'd be
the next brown girl to read the news. She had
the accent (learned) and her opportunity:
a friend who got there through her dad.
But my sister wanted to make it on her own
– till now. For here's a picture of her, electrocuted;
plunging, into ice-cold water; and here she is at the finish line.
I can't believe you pay for this, I tell her.
She says it's about helping each other
over the obstacles. My sister, who fought and defeated my father
and mother's hope we'd be doctors (before I was born)
laughs, comparing you to the Yorkshireman
she wed. What it means, and takes, to be, and love, a person!

This is not a photograph

– a poem is never a photograph
like this one you took of rain-glittering Wall Street
after the shooting blocks from our
hotel – and the morning's downpour –
in it I eat crab rangoon. Fake crab meat;
real cream cheese; American Chinese:
to be dipped in a tub of lurid sauce
like back in the heartland with a woman twice
my age (with two kids) I'd met online.
The internet I like to imagine
was different then. 'Random chat'
with a stranger from anywhere – I call that
utopian. A taste of my past in the centre of power
– no you didn't want any but took the picture.

47

Faraj

How to speak the name – trochee
or iamb – of the coolest man I'd ever met;
who wore, in the Tunisian heat, a pale-gold, glittering suit?
The translator sat between Faraj and me
on the gorgeous balcony, where the flies were fewer.
Stumped smiles, gestures, recognition. Faraj
was Libyan. Militia rule; rocket fire
diverted his flight to Tripoli. But I was there
to English his poems of love-struck, unironical passion
in which none of this appeared. I couldn't help
but lend each perfumed, elusive lover
your ached-for silhouette… Carefully, after an explanation,
he put into Arabic my small poem about small people: repression
and fear in the country of Nigel Farage.

It's a dark

blue, your new winter coat – shapelier
than the last. A girl with brown hair,
wearing it, gazes at the river.
Her forearms repose on Arup's concrete.
– I thought she was you, for a moment
stymied by that navy silhouette.
And there's your name. Everywhere,
unlike mine. Pinned to the breast of a stranger;
spoken by another in the street.
Again – by the library's glass door –
that coat. That hair. If I could see her face
would it vanish, this startled sweetness?
Of course the coat comes off. It's on trend.
The stranger walks off with her friend.

48

Whoever you are

I have always depended on the kindness
of strangers: by which I don't just mean,
bussing it on the Whey-Aye Five-0
to a school I'd never visited, the terse,
unsmiling, helpful, flat-capped gentleman
who told me where exactly to get off
and through the grimed window
raised his hand in salutation; or the driver of the bus,
who when I pressed the bell too soon
joked, softly, 'not too many get down here';
but the faceless driver of the motor,
who, as I plodged in the wrong direction
up a gelid A-road through the knee-high grass
horned, to let me know – I know that was the reason.

Haircut

I'm touched by the Italian's scissors
and the story of his granny
who, in service down south, sent money
home to her family of miners. He listens
to what I say of Durham; and disagrees.
'It's like the United Nations,' he grins. The Chinese
he loves for their sense of honour
means a haircut before going home, and not after...
But they can't say no. To save face (theirs or his?)
when he asks 'is this good for you?' they whisper yes
– then want more off! Saudis
hunt a nuance over which to quibble
and one was shocked to hear
of his divorce. 'How could you do such a thing to her?!'

My parents and I

speak of how we got here;
like bodies they pile up, the anecdotes. Later,
the electric toothbrush dies. One couldn't find a better
example of a 'first world problem'; though you'll remember
my thigh burned by our towel rail. It was torture.
On the brink of my return
to my true home, the one in which we live,
I touch the dry tome that lives on the cistern
– about our civil war – and feel as if
I could be anyone on this earth, or no one.
Except those gun-jostled in the lumbar curve
or dripped on through a shack of corrugated metal
or studying in cadjan huts by the weak glow of coconut oil
have no clean white space, do they, in which to shit.

My Sri Lankan family

extends its electronic tentacles across the ocean.
From the outskirts of Sydney, my cousin
Skypes my uncle in Colombo every day.
My parents live in Leeds, just two hours away,
but here they are, trying to fix the mic.
She tells you at length about her divorced friend
who's lonely and whose dog began to bite:
'Its name was Willow, it was a long WILLOW-type dog.'
Crisply, he explains: 'It's a greyhound.'
They're keen to know our plans. Someone has wed
'another Tamil, and of the same caste. Just like back
at home – it's so primitive – on our small island:
is the girl even happy?' And my mother: 'you do not know that,
they are VERY VERY ASIANS. She is on my Facebook.'

Swedenborg

His more-than-glimpse of what occurs
in heaven amounts, says
Lagercrantz, to not the truth but 'a poem
about a foreign country with peculiar laws and customs'.
We will be married for all time and space.
There is no dominion in that place
where the neighbourhood of angels is changed
by what they think and feel in the crucible
of the moment. But for the moment
when you make your bid for my touch
and, for some reason, I go on stroking my way
through Wikipedia, it's like what he calls hell:
the nation our lives choose, and which we may
elect to leave at any time, but never will.

Union

When you ask me to close my eyes I only
turn on my side and touch my phone.
The sound of the sea from a distance is lonely
and as the fabric of the informal, off-white dress
you'll marry me in slides over your skin
what I can hear but not see is furious foam
breaking, near the horizon, where there's
a swatch of sunlight, over glimpsed rock.
I'm talking to you, and someone is listening in,
of a certain or uncertain politics. Whose line
am I repeating or crossing or about to colour
outside now a voice says 'You can look'?
It's with your love I try to love that stranger
who walked so far to read this page.

It's not about you

says lover to lover; and writer, to writer.
We let each other down, then up. Is this corner
yours or mine that we find ourselves in; and do
crises really touch the truth, above and beyond our everyday joy?
In the film, the robot from the future is programmed to say
come with me if you want to live.
Swap the first and last words around, love.
Inside my ring I read the words you had engraved.
I do not think two people could be so happy.
I want and do not want everyone to feel this way
and each moment with you is abrim. – But I do go on,
don't I – leading, with two left feet – why press
on the reader one half of a conversation?
For no one could ever take your place.

Barrett/Browning

Fake news stays news. It inspires.
A sort of muse. A sumptuous invitation
to look violently. Gently we plan
our wedding, insisting we don't care
too much about the bouquets or the food
– parents can't fathom our present need
to laugh things off and be small scale.
For years, he told her, I ate like Shelley
only bread and potatoes. It was the day
after September 11. They didn't elope
though disapproval followed them to Paris.
They married secretly in Marylebone
witnessed by a maid and cousin. A leap
not of faith, but the imagination. This is news to me.

In the bubble

– the echo chamber, the centrally-heated slump
of Sunday afternoon, we've the TV
flaring, and our tinsel. Cosy
beneath a red-blue blanket, we're made to jump
by a blank and searching face at the pane.
It's your friend come round for Christmas carols.
Jaggedly as you fetch your violin
she gives us – with a smile – both barrels
having tried the door already and your silenced phone.
We thank her for Thanksgiving. She explains:
when we were late they grew afraid,
she and her husband, that we wouldn't come
for though her postal vote was for Hillary, he went for Trump.
Everyone is talking about and not to them.

The hearing aid

Ma says she'll think about beginning to one day
consider getting one, perhaps – when she's eighty.
We both struggle with hot cross-talk,
our ears were built for one and not congested,
overlapping conversations. There are plenty
like us. My hearing's fine. I've been tested
and they found it's just the human voice
I struggle to pick out from background noise.
What's the difference? We are the universe
evolved to the point of considering itself. Talking
to itself. Last night I had, you say, an argument
in my sleep. I know it was broken. Was
it the mattress? You offer to switch sides.
When I begin to shout, I use long words.

New Year's Eve

I'm sitting downstairs in the silent house,
reading, for the first time in weeks
– it's Raymond Carver. In what looks
a painful position your father sleeps. Hours
later, your brother's wife, following confession,
says, in her melodic style – she's Romanian –
it is so quiet in this house, I thought you all
had gone away. I know that feeling so well.
Yesterday, how could I have abandoned
my predictions? Yet even the expected will
shine tomorrow with a quality we don't command.
I worry, therefore I am. But do we really have
to square these moments of astonishment
with the responsibilities of our life?

Driving

to Galle, to you, after a week apart
I feel kindly towards the island:
streaked concrete, towers of gods, glittering sand.
I lost you. On the phone, so many times. White noise.
Underwater distortion. My heart,
and the sea, and the crickets, the only sound
as we spoke into the dark and neither voice
came through. Yet here, in the rational daylight,
is the Maliban factory, whose gutter ran pink with sugar;
whose lemon biscuits, years before I was born
sustained my family during the cyclone. A motorbike
with a girl in a green sari riding postilion.
The vent's cool air touches my face
and stung forearms, lightly as your kiss.

This book

claims eczema like yours, that comes and goes
like ambition or lust or cloud shadow on gorse
is its own explanation. The body's morse
for hurts words cannot touch. I've
scratched – you disapprove – these ant
bites to raw calderas – moats of hives;
red, flashing buttons. When I can sleep I can't
help it! You dab cream on the ankle cyst
the doctor wishes to excise and send away
despite the sunshield of my pigment.
Just in case. Are the cells I am given
to friendly fire? Civil war is what cancer is,
a suborning of one's own deep forces.
Your moles amaze me like stars in the sky.

Mother and sister

Waist-deep in zinnias by the window,
one cradles the other. The photo's
black-and-white, faded, seems oddly Victorian.
Except these are my people. I don't know
the colour of the bands of plaster
standing proud of the wall that's rubble now.
Someone, somewhere, is a wound
speaking. An ear, listening. 'I can imagine,'
comes the reply. Souls touch only
as stems and petals are half-perceived
through a sari's silk. As thoughts of the real
world's harms haunt the child in her mother's arms.
We look and look until we almost feel
the past's no foreign country after all.

The X-Files

– Binged on legally, thanks to one
Leviathan of tax avoidance. Scully deplores
these trips from the centre of power
into the heartland: 'They don't want anything
to do with us.' The week before
the election, nothing was left for us
to see at Vindolanda but the bare,
military foundations. 'Mulder, the truth is out there
but so are lies.' We walked at sunset
a blue-red residue of Hadrian's big,
unbeautiful wall. Mulder listens
cannily, in Sioux City, Idaho
to a bartender with a burned-off ear
and a tattoo of a flying saucer.

Contrarieties

I take both Blakes – Daniel, and William –
at their word. One of them imagined
a place *where no dispute could ever come.*
Your engagement ring you've left behind
to keep both you and it from harm. The band
meets in Byker, where it's grim. Blake
grappled with an abstruse system
heroically. You searched online for others; found them.
Each time you'd rather stay at home with me
but don't. That's innocence. That's experience. Tony,
a paramedic, is your lift back
to the station. He once retrieved a stillbirth from a toilet bowl.
Some to misery are born. The image is engraved.
Lines the burin made – your violin strings – begin to howl.

In films

– they've an agenda, of course – couples
read instead of having sex. To read in bed
is to be alone, and timorous, in that place
domestic bodies should be wed.
Cinema requires its shorthand, its givens
that sum us up in just so many scenes.
But I can't stand the director's knowing look
for when we sit together, both with a book,
solitudes meld – as between the sheets – lamplight
warms the thigh-smooth page. If a bit
is beautiful, or bad, or funny, we read it out.
Turning the page, you laugh, leaving me
to ask what's going on, or not – lingering
like a passionfruit's long, gum-piercing, pang.

We're moving on

– Our fourth move in as many years.
Where and for what will we ever settle?
The clothes horse is chock-a-block; as we ball
our rainbow of socks into pairs
I want to hold the moment, gently as a petal,
between my finger and thumb. But this house
is home to you, and so you have it worse;
a loved nook that will leave a bruise.
– Where I can look at you is where my home is.
As we uproot blade-clogging moss
(will our next place have a garden?),
you mention my brother-in-law. He's brown-green
colourblind: my sister's flesh is grass.
The odour of summer climbs into bed with us.

Birmingham

A clatter in the pre-dawn hours.
Half-asleep, mumbling to each other
out of our private dreams we decide
it's no intruder, but the noise outside
of glass bottles toppling into a skip.
– But that was our Durham flat opposite the club,
three years ago. A shelf in the kitchen
has given way and scattered maple syrup,
glass, flour, oats, sugar, everywhere.
The peed-on stick said three weeks in.
You were afraid last night we'd crush the life within;
today, you said, there were waves of emotion
– as you edged barefoot between the gooey shards
determined to, at once, alone, clean up.

...of justice

We'd felt inhuman and a bit guilty, for
what others go on struggling for
was given us (it seemed) in just one go.
Bishop tore into Lowell for the talk show
he made of his ex-wife's letters – exposing her
and, vainly, himself. I wish your voice,
its strength, intelligence, kindness
could enter into mine, like a new life. You are
so good to me, to everyone, to strangers online:
'No one explains that it's so common,
but if you search, many lost theirs early on:
Six weeks in and can't stop crying.
Every time I go to the loo. I don't know
how long it will continue. But this is happening to you too.'

Trying

to unpeel the bin bag's clingy sides
was like the squinch of failing to remember
the name of an old friend, my own new number,
or the terrors of last spring – between me and you
asquat by the gate deadheading and uprooting
those green explosions through mauve shale.
Into fissures ants fled the genocide.
Blown dandelion clocks appeared
like aliens or desiccated jellyfish
atop the red-stained stems you poured
in the black hole glowing between my thighs.
The letterbox letters have buffed to
if not a mirror then a curry-ready steel plate
sparkled like a Howard Hodgkin.

Artist

When you were young you'd draw and paint.
Then your brother said all you could do
was copy down what was in front of you.
So you stopped. Sometimes you start again.
He's bought you watercolours. He is a saint
but what's done is done. I don't,
for more than a rearriving moment,
understand. For his role in your family was mine
in mine. How could I never learn,
till watching you, what sketching means:
touching with your eyes what has been given
again, and again, and again. It's the way you were raised.
The way you were erased. But I envy your line
that self-forgetful vigilance – its hesitation, even.

It must be

I got to thinking no one could hear
my voice – all too possible to ignore
at work and play – or see my brown face
without a twinge of…something – How scandalous,
for me to be working and living there!
Abuse in the street and a poisoned office
– the feeling of unsafety which my folk
flew across the ocean or found on arrival
grew, while I wasn't watching, skin deep.
(Nothing is so deep as skin, so archival.)
Reteaching my words to not give up,
your face, unshocked, undismayed, by mine,
gave the brightness back to my reflection.
The gift was everything, and gradual.

Spring

On waking, you draw the blossoms
of the plum tree to my attention.
Last time it flowered we weren't yet here.
During the night, your pyjama bottoms
slipped down. Something to mention.
'Isn't it beautiful?' is what you're asking.
'Yes,' is my reply to you forever
whether or not we're looking at the same thing
or in the same direction. To ask that
must be frightening. What if I said no,
or crinkled up my nose? The flower's
tiny, white, countless. How; why? I have
no explanation. It's too much. You are in
agreement. They are in touch. We are in love.